The Gospel of Emerson

by
Newton Dillaway

UNITY BOOKS
Unity Village, MO 64065

Fourteenth Edition

1990 — Unity Books — Sixth Hardcover Printing

UNITY SCHOOL OF CHRISTIANITY
Unity Village, MO 64065

ISBN-0-87159-046-8

This book is printed on recycled paper.

CONTENTS

To

Edward Waldo Forbes

Who through the years has helped and
encouraged those engaged in spreading
the message of his grandfather,
Ralph Waldo Emerson

Foreword

This volume may be seen as a digest of Emerson's spiritual gospel. It is not easy to detect this gospel, for it is hidden in a hundred essays, letters, poems, notes; and in many entries of the journals. After years of study and thought, and consultation with other students of Emerson, the gospel herein presented has gradually emerged from some twenty-five volumes of the seer's writings. The main objectives were to bring out the cardinal points of the subject under consideration, and to arrange the quotations in some semblance of order and progression. But even these objectives were subordinated to the aspiration to give something that would really open up the inner life of the sensitive reader.

Virtually all of the text is direct quotation from the essays, journals, poems, letters and manuscript notes of Ralph Waldo Emerson. The small amount of thought in italics is my own, unless otherwise designated. All the rest is quotation from Emerson. Sources will be found on page 124.

The general tenor of Emerson's philosophy seemed to me to indicate the advisability of keeping even the seer himself in the background. "The soul knows no persons."

The great majority of the quotations are from the Centenary Edition of Emerson's works. These are reprinted by permission of, and by arrangement with, Houghton Mifflin Company. The final selection in the chapter on the soul is from *A Letter of Emerson* (The Beacon Press) and is reprinted by permission of Mr. Willard Reed, the editor of the volume. I am indebted to Dr. Arthur P. Moor and to my wife, Hope Dillaway, for assistance in preparing the original text. I wish to thank Mr. Edward W. Forbes, Mrs. Raymond Emerson, Mrs. Alexander Golitzen and Vida Reed Stone for their interest and help.

NEWTON DILLAWAY

The Coming of the Spirit

In those days there arose a Prophet—a Prophet of the New World.

Earlier the Light was not up. But one day the Creative Spirit spoke to the young man and commissioned him as follows:

Thou shalt not profess that which thou dost not believe.

Thou shalt not heed the voice of man when it agrees not with the voice of God in thine own soul.

Thou shalt study and obey the laws of the Universe, and they will be thy fellow servants.

Nature shall be to thee as a symbol. The life of the soul in conscious union with the Infinite shall be for thee the only real existence.

Teach men that each generation begins the world afresh, in perfect freedom; that the present is not the prisoner of the past, but that to-day holds captive all the yesterdays, to judge, to accept, to reject their teachings, as they are shown by its own morning sun.

To thy fellow countrymen thou shalt preach the gospel of the New World, that here, here in America, is the home of man, that here is the promise of a new and more excellent social state than history has recorded.

Earlier the Light was not always clear. Should he serve Tradition or the Presence? Should he serve traditional religion or the religion of the seers? And what is religion?

Pondering these problems, the young man retired to the mountains to meditate.

Here, among the mountains, the pinions of thought should be strong, and one should see the errors of men from a calmer height of love and wisdom. What is the message that is given me to communicate next Sunday? Religion in the mind is not credulity, and in the practice is not form. It is a life. It is the order and soundness of a man. It is not something else *to be got,* to be *added,* but is a new life of those faculties you have. It is to do right. It is to love, it is to serve, it is to think, it is to be humble.

Having turned to the practice of the seers, it was perhaps inevitable that the young man should be led to the Way of the seers. He broke with Tradition and chose the Way of Insight.

Having been untuned by Fate, the young man went to the Old World to seek equilibrium in new surroundings and from new minds. The result was an awakening that gave him fresh confidence in himself. The minds of the Old World did not move him to any great extent.

I thank the Great God who has led me through this European scene, this last school-room in which he has pleased to instruct me, from Malta's isle, through Sicily, through Italy, through Switzerland, through France, through England, through Scotland, in safety and pleasure, and has now brought me to the shore and the ship that steers westward. He has shown me the men I wished to see,—Landor, Coleridge, Carlyle, Wordsworth; he has thereby comforted and confirmed me in my convictions. Many things I owe to the sight of these men. I shall judge more justly, less timidly, of wise men forevermore. To be sure not one of these is a mind of the very first class, but what the intercourse with each of these suggests is true of intercourse with better men, that they never *fill the ear*—fill

the mind—no, it is an *idealized* portrait which
always we draw of them. Upon an intelligent
man, wholly a stranger to their names, they
would make in conversation no deep impression,
none of a world-filling fame,—they would be
remembered as sensible, well-read, earnest men,
not more. Especially are they all deficient, all
these four,—in different degrees, but all deficient,—in insight into religious truth. They
have no idea of that species of moral truth which
I call the first philosophy. . . .

*As the young man returned to the New
World, the Creative Spirit spoke again.*

Let us hear this new thing. It is very old.
It is the old revelation, that perfect beauty is
perfect goodness, it is the development of the
wonderful congruities of the moral law of human nature. Let me enumerate a few of the re-
markable properties of that nature. A man contains all that is needful to his government within
himself. He is made a law unto himself. All
real good or evil that can befall him must be
from himself. . . . The purpose of life seems
to be to acquaint a man with himself. He is not
to live to the future as described to him, but
to live to the real future by living to the real
present. The highest revelation is that God is
in every man.

With the coming of this oracle, the young

*man rose into the Creative Consciousness and
began to speak as a Prophet. He was henceforth
to serve as a vehicle for Insight in moulding a
gospel of the New World.*

As God *liveth*

> The word unto the prophet spoken
> Was writ on tables yet unbroken;
> Still floats upon the morning wind,
> Still whispers to the willing mind.

Religion

1. I was made very sensible of the desire of all open minds for religious teaching. The young men and . . . women freely expressed to me their wish for more light . . . the inquiry and the tone of these inquirers showed plainly what one may easily see in Boston and Cambridge and the villages also—that what men want is a Religion.

2. Religion is the emotion of reverence which the presence of the universal mind ever excites in the individual.

3. Now the first position I make is that natural religion supplies still all the facts which

are disguised under the dogma of popular creeds.

4. We are all believers in natural religion; we all agree that the health and integrity of man is self-respect, self-subsistency, a regard to natural conscience. All education is to accustom him to trust himself, discriminate between his higher and lower thoughts, exert the timid faculties until they are robust, and thus train him to self-help, until he ceases to be an underling, a tool, and becomes a benefactor. I think wise men wish their religion to be all of this kind, teaching the agent to go alone, not to hang on the world as a pensioner, a permitted person, but an adult, self-searching soul, brave to assist or resist a world: only humble and docile before the source of the wisdom he has discovered within him.

5. You say there is no religion now. 'Tis like saying in rainy weather, There is no sun, when at that moment we are witnessing one of his superlative effects. The religion of the cultivated class now, to be sure, consists in an avoidance of acts and engagements which it was once their religion to assume. But this avoidance will yield spontaneous forms in their due hour.

6. The multitude of the sick shall not make us deny the existence of health. In spite of our imbecility and terrors, and "universal decay of

religion," etc., etc., the moral sense reappears to-day with the same morning newness that has been from of old the fountain of beauty and strength.

7. There is a principle which is the basis of things, which all speech aims to say, and all action to evolve, a simple, quiet, undescribed, undescribable presence, dwelling very peacefully in us, our rightful lord: we are not to do, but to let do; not to work, but to be worked upon; and to this homage there is a consent of all thoughtful and just men in all ages and conditions. To this sentiment belong vast and sudden enlargements of power. . . . we are one day to deal with real being,—essences with essences.

8. As the religious sentiment is the most vital and sublime of all our sentiments, and capable of the most prodigious effects, so is it abhorrent to our whole nature, when, in the absence of the sentiment, the act or word or officer volunteers to stand in its stead.

9. In religion, the sentiment is all; the ritual or ceremony indifferent. But the inertia of men inclines them, when the sentiment sleeps, to imitate that thing it did; it goes through the ceremony omitting only the will, makes the mistake of the wig for the head, the clothes for the man.

10. Instead of that reliance which the soul

suggests, on the eternity of truth and duty, men are misled into a reliance on institutions, which, the moment they cease to be the instantaneous creations of the devout sentiment, are worthless. Religion among the low becomes low. As it loses its truth, it loses credit with the sagacious.

11. I think the necessity very great, and it has prompted an equal magnanimity, that thus invites all classes, all religious men, whatever their connections, whatever their specialties, in whatever relation they stand to the Christian Church, to unite in a movement of benefit to men, under the sanction of religion. We are all very sensible—it is forced on us every day—of the feeling that . . . the creeds are outgrown; that a technical theology no longer suits us. It is not the ill will of people—no, indeed, but the incapacity for confining themselves there.

12. Religion is the relation of the soul to God, and therefore the progress of Sectarianism marks the decline of religion. For, looking at God instantly reduces our disposition to dissent from our brother. A man may die by a fever as well as by consumption, and religion is as effectually destroyed by bigotry as by indifference.

13. I suppose it is not wise, not being natural, to belong to any religious party. In the Bible you are not directed to be a Unitarian, or a Calvinist or an Episcopalian. . . . As fast as

any man becomes great, that is, thinks, he becomes a new party. Socrates, Aristotle, Calvin, Luther, Abelard, what are these but names of parties? Which is to say, As fast as we use our own eyes, we quit these parties or Unthinking Corporations, and join ourselves to God in an unpartaken relation.

14. Is it not true that contemplation belongs to us, and therefore outward worship, *because* our reason is at discord with our understanding? And that, whenever we live rightly, thought will express itself in ordinary action so fully as to make a special action, that is, a religious form, impertinent? Is not Solomon's temple built because Solomon is not a temple, but a brothel and a change-house? Is not the meeting-house dedicated because men are not? . . . when he who worships there, speaks the truth, follows the truth, is the truth's; when he awakes by actual communion to the faith that God is in him, will he need any temple, any prayer? . . . Now does this sound like high treason and go to lay flat all religion? It does threaten our forms; but does not that very word 'form' already sound hollow? It threatens our forms, but it does not touch injuriously Religion. Would there be danger if there were real religion? If the doctrine that God is in man were faithfully taught and received, if I lived to speak the truth and

enact it, if I pursued every generous sentiment as one enamoured, if the majesty of goodness were reverenced, would not such a principle serve me by way of police at least as well as a Connecticut Sunday?

15. America shall introduce a pure religion.

16. There will be a new church founded on moral science; at first cold and naked, a babe in a manger again, the algebra and mathematics of ethical law, the church of men to come, without shawms, or psaltery, or sackbut; but it will have heaven and earth for its beams and rafters; science for symbol and illustration; it will fast enough gather beauty, music, picture, poetry. Was never stoicism so stern and exigent as this shall be. It shall send man home to his central solitude, shame these social, supplicating manners, and make him know that much of the time he must have himself to his friend. He shall expect no co-operation, he shall walk with no companion. The nameless Thought, the nameless Power, the super-personal Heart,—he shall repose alone on that. He needs only his own verdict. No good fame can help, no bad fame can hurt him. The Laws are his consolers, the good Laws themselves are alive, they know if he have kept them, they animate him with the leading of great duty, and an endless horizon.

The Way

1. Let me admonish you, first of all, to go alone; to refuse the good models, even those which are sacred in the imagination of men, and dare to love God without mediator or veil.

2. Yourself a newborn bard of the Holy Ghost, cast behind you all conformity, and acquaint men at first hand with Deity. Look to it first and only, that fashion, custom, authority, pleasure, and money, are nothing to you,—are not bandages over your eyes, that you cannot see, —but live with the privilege of the immeasurable mind.

3. Nothing is secure but life, transition,

the energizing spirit. No love can be bound by oath or covenant to secure it against a higher love. No truth so sublime but it may be trivial tomorrow in the light of new thoughts. People wish to be settled; only as far as they are unsettled is there any hope for them.

4. We do not guess to-day the mood, the pleasure, the power of to-morrow, when we are building up our being. Of lower states, of acts of routine and sense, we can tell somewhat; but the masterpieces of God, the total growths and universal movements of the soul, he hideth; they are incalculable. I can know that truth is divine and helpful; but how it shall help me I can have no guess, for *so to be* is the sole inlet of *so to know.* The new position of the advancing man has all the powers of the old, yet has them all new. It carries in its bosom all the energies of the past, yet is itself an exhalation of the morning. I cast away in this new moment all my once hoarded knowledge, as vacant and vain. Now for the first time seem I to know any thing rightly.

5. The soul gives itself, alone, original and pure, to the Lonely, Original, and Pure, who, on that condition, gladly inhabits, leads and speaks through it. Then is it glad, young and nimble. It is not wise, but it sees through all things. It is not called religious, but it is in-

nocent. It calls the light its own, and feels that the grass grows and the stone falls by a law inferior to, and dependent on, its nature. Behold, it saith, I am born into the great, the universal mind. I, the imperfect, adore my own Perfect. I am somehow receptive óf the great soul, and thereby I do overlook the sun and the stars and feel them to be the fair accidents and effects which change and pass. More and more the surges of everlasting nature enter into me, and I become public and human in my regards and actions. So come I to live in thoughts and act with energies which are immortal. Thus revering the soul, and learning, as the ancient said, that "its beauty is immense," man will come to see that the world is the perennial miracle which the soul worketh, and be less astonished at particular wonders; he will learn that there is no profane history; that all history is sacred; that the universe is represented in an atom, in a moment of time. He will weave no longer a spotted life of shreds and patches, but he will live with a divine unity. He will cease from what is base and frivolous in his life and be content with all places and with any service he can render. He will calmly front the morrow in the negligency of that trust which carries God with it and so hath already the whole future in the bottom of the heart.

6. Nothing great was ever achieved without enthusiasm. The way of life is wonderful; it is by abandonment. The great moments of history are the facilities of performance through the strength of ideas, as the works of genius and religion. "A man," said Oliver Cromwell, "never rises so high as when he knows not whither he is going."

7. We do not yet see that virtue is Height, and that a man or a company of men, plastic and permeable to principles, by the law of nature must overpower and ride all cities, nations, kings, rich men, poets, who are not.

8. We are wiser than we know. If we will not interfere with our thought, but will act entirely, or see how the thing stands in God, we know the particular thing, and every thing, and every man. For the Maker of all things and all persons stands behind us and casts his dread omniscience through us over things.

9. The soul's communication of truth is the highest event in nature, since it then does not give somewhat from itself, but it gives itself, or passes into and becomes that man whom it enlightens; or in proportion to that truth he receives, it takes him to itself.

10. This communication is an influx of the Divine mind into our mind.

11. In these communications the power to

see is not separated from the will to do, but
the insight proceeds from obedience, and the
obedience proceeds from a joyful perception.
Every moment when the individual feels himself invaded by it is memorable. By the necessity
of our constitution a certain enthusiasm attends
the individual's consciousness of that divine
presence.

12. The nature of these revelations is the
same; they are perceptions of the absolute law.
They are solutions of the soul's own questions.
They do not answer the questions which the
understanding asks. The soul answers never by
words, but by the thing itself that is inquired
after.

13. Revelation is the disclosure of the soul.
The popular notion of a revelation is that it is
a telling of fortunes. In past oracles of the soul
the understanding seeks to find answers to
sensual questions, and undertakes to tell from
God how long men shall exist, what their hands
shall do and who shall be their company, add-
ing names and dates and places. But we must
pick no locks. We must check this low curiosity.

14. These questions which we lust to ask
about the future are a confession of sin. God
has no answer for them. No answer in words
can reply to a question of things. It is not in
an arbitrary "decree of God," but in the nature

of man, that a veil shuts down on the facts of to-morrow; for the soul will not have us read any other cipher than that of cause and effect. By this veil which curtains events it instructs the children of men to live in to-day. The only mode of obtaining an answer to these questions of the senses is to forego all low curiosity, and, accepting the tide of being which floats us into the secret of nature, work and live, work and live, and all unawares the advancing soul has built and forged for itself a new condition, and the question and the answer are one.

Soul

1. There is one soul.

    It is related to the world.

    Art is its action thereon.

    Science finds its methods.

    Literature is its record.

    Religion is the emotion of reverence that it inspires.

    Ethics is the soul illustrated in human life.

    Society is the finding of this soul by individuals in each other.

    Trades are the learning of the soul in nature by labor.

Politics is the activity of the soul illustrated in power.

Manners are silent and mediate expressions of soul.

2. The Supreme Critic on the errors of the past and the present, and the only prophet of that which must be, is that great nature in which we rest as the earth lies in the soft arms of the atmosphere; that Unity, that Over-Soul, within which every man's particular being is contained and made one with all other; that common heart of which all sincere conversation is the worship, to which all right action is submission; that overpowering reality which confutes our tricks and talents, and constrains every one to pass for what he is, and to speak from his character and not from his tongue, and which evermore tends to pass into our thought and hand and become wisdom and virtue and power and beauty. We live in succession, in division, in parts, in particles. Meantime within man is the soul of the whole; the wise silence; the universal beauty, to which every part and particle is equally related; the eternal ONE. And this deep power in which we exist and whose beatitude is all accessible to us, is not only self-sufficing and perfect in every hour, but the act of seeing and the thing seen, the seer and the spectacle, the subject and the object, are one.

3. All goes to show that the soul in man is not an organ, but animates and exercises all the organs; is not a function, like the power of memory, of calculation, of comparison, but uses these as hands and feet; is not a faculty, but a light; is not the intellect or the will, but the master of the intellect and the will; is the background of our being, in which they lie,—an immensity not possessed and that cannot be possessed. From within or from behind, a light shines through us upon things and makes us aware that we are nothing, but the light is all.

4. What we commonly call man, the eating, drinking, planting, counting man, does not, as we know him, represent himself, but misrepresents himself. Him we do not respect, but the soul, whose organ he is, would he let it appear through his action, would make our knees bend. When it breathes through his intellect, it is genius; when it breathes through his will, it is virtue; when it flows through his affection, it is love. And the blindness of the intellect begins when it would be something of itself. The weakness of the will begins when the individual would be something of himself. All reform aims in some one particular to let the soul have its way through us; in other words, to engage us to obey.

5. Language cannot paint it with his colors.

It is too subtile. It is undefinable, unmeasurable; but we know that it pervades and contains us. We know that all spiritual being is in man. A wise old proverb says, "God comes to see us without bell;" that is, as there is no screen or ceiling between our heads and the infinite heavens, so is there no bar or wall in the soul, where man, the effect, ceases, and God, the cause, begins. The walls are taken away. We lie open on one side to the deeps of spiritual nature, to the attributes of God. Justice we see and know, Love, Freedom, Power. These natures no man ever got above, but they tower over us, and most in the moment when our interests tempt us to wound them.

6. After its own law and not by arithmetic is the rate of its progress to be computed. The soul's advances are not made by gradation, such as can be represented by motion in a straight line, but rather by ascension of state, such as can be represented by metamorphosis,—from the egg to the worm, from the worm to the fly.

7. Philosophically considered, the universe is composed of Nature and the Soul. Strictly speaking, therefore, all that is separate from us, all which Philosophy distinguishes as the NOT ME, that is, both nature and art, all other men and my own body, must be ranked under this name, NATURE.

8. The life of man is a self-evolving circle, which, from a ring imperceptibly small, rushes on all sides outwards to new and larger circles, and that without end. The extent to which this generation of circles, wheel without wheel, will go, depends on the force or truth of the individual soul. For it is the inert effort of each thought, having formed itself into a circular wave of circumstance,—as for instance an empire, rules of an art, a local usage, a religious rite,—to heap itself on that ridge and to solidify and hem in the life. But if the soul is quick and strong it bursts over that boundary on all sides and expands another orbit on the great deep, which also runs up into a high wave, with attempt again to stop and to bind. But the heart refuses to be imprisoned; in its first and narrowest pulses it already tends outward with a vast force and to immense and innumerable expansions.

9. Step by step we scale this mysterious ladder; the steps are actions, the new prospect is power. Every several result is threatened and judged by that which follows. Every one seems to be contradicted by the new; it is only limited by the new. The new statement is always hated by the old, and, to those dwelling in the old, comes like an abyss of scepticism. But the eye soon gets wonted to it, for the eye and it are effects of one cause; then its innocency and bene-

fit appear, and presently, all its energy spent, it pales and dwindles before the revelation of the new hour.

10. Shall I say then that as far as we can trace the natural history of the soul, its health consists in the fulness of its reception?—call it piety, call it veneration,—in the fact that enthusiasm is organized therein. What is best in any work of art but that part which the work itself seems to require and do; that which the man cannot do again; that which flows from the hour and the occasion, like the eloquence of men in a tumultuous debate?

11. We cannot describe the natural history of the soul, but we know that it is divine. I cannot tell if these wonderful qualities which house to-day in this mortal frame shall ever re-assemble in equal activity in a similar frame, or whether they have before had a natural history like that of this body you see before you; but this one thing I know, that these qualities did not now begin to exist, cannot be sick with my sickness, nor buried in any grave; but that they circulate through the Universe: before the world was, they were. Nothing can bar them out, or shut them in, but they penetrate the ocean and land, space and time, form and essence, and hold the key to universal nature.

12. Excite the soul, and it becomes suddenly

virtuous. Touch the deep heart, and all these listless, stingy, beef-eating by-standers will see the dignity of a sentiment; will say, This is good, and all I have I will give for that. Excite the soul, and the weather and the town and your condition in the world all disappear; the world itself loses its solidity, nothing remains but the soul and the Divine Presence in which it lives.

13. As soon as every man is apprised of the Divine Presence within his own mind,—is apprised that the perfect law of duty corresponds with the laws of chemistry, of vegetation, of astronomy, as face to face in a glass; that the basis of duty, the order of society, the power of character, the wealth of culture, the perfection of taste, all draw their essence from this moral sentiment, then we have a religion that exalts, that commands all the social and all the private action.

14. The relations of the soul to the divine spirit are so pure that it is profane to seek to interpose helps. It must be that when God speaketh he should communicate, not one thing, but all things; should fill the world with his voice; should scatter forth light, nature, time, souls, from the centre of the present thought; and new date and new create the whole. Whenever a mind is simple and receives a divine wisdom,

old things pass away,—means, teachers, texts,
temples fall; it lives now, and absorbs past and
future into the present hour. All things are
made sacred by relation to it,—one as much as
another. All things are dissolved to their centre
by their cause, and in the universal miracle petty
and particular miracles disappear. If therefore
a man claims to know and speak of God and
carries you backward to the phraseology of some
old mouldered nation in another country, in
another world, believe him not. Is the acorn
better than the oak which is its fulness and com-
pletion? Is the parent better than the child into
whom he has cast his ripened being? Whence
then this worship of the past? The centuries are
conspirators against the sanity and authority of
the soul. Time and space are but physiological
colors which the eye makes, but the soul is light:
where it is, is day; where it was, is night; and
history is an impertinence and an injury if it be
any thing more than a cheerful apologue or
parable of my being and becoming.

15. So that I count these to be low, sleepy,
dark ages of the Soul, only redeemed by the
unceasing affirmation at the bottom of the heart
—like the nightingale's song heard all night—
that the powers of the Soul are commensurate
with its needs, all experience to the contrary
notwithstanding.

Mind

1. There is one mind common to all individual men. Every man is an inlet to the same and to all of the same. He that is once admitted to the right of reason is made a freeman of the whole estate. What Plato has thought, he may think; what a saint has felt, he may feel; what at any time has befallen any man, he can understand. Who hath access to this universal mind is a party to all that is or can be done, for this is the only and sovereign agent.

2. Mind is the only reality, of which men and all other natures are better or worse reflectors.

3. I am of the oldest religion. Leaving aside the question which was prior, egg or bird, I believe the mind is the creator of the world, and is ever creating;—that at last Matter is dead Mind; that mind makes the senses it sees with; that the genius of man is a continuation of the power that made him and that has not done making him.

I dare not deal with this element in its pure essence. It is too rare for the wings of words. Yet I see that Intellect is a science of degrees, and that as man is conscious of the law of vegetable and animal nature, so he is aware of an Intellect which overhangs his consciousness like a sky, of degree above degree, of heaven within heaven.

Every just thinker has attempted to indicate these degrees, these steps on the heavenly stair, until he comes to light where language fails him. Above the thought is the higher truth,— truth as yet undomesticated and therefore un-formulated.

4. Of the perception now fast becoming a conscious fact,—that there is One Mind, and that all the powers and privileges which lie in any, lie in all; that I, as a man, may claim and appropriate whatever of true or fair or good or strong has anywhere been exhibited; that Moses and Confucius, Montaigne and Leibnitz, are

not so much individuals as they are parts of man and parts of me, and my intelligence proves them my own,—literature is far the best expression.

5. A mind does not receive truth as a chest receives jewels that are put into it, but as the stomach takes up food into the system. It is no longer food, but flesh, and is assimilated. The appetite and the power of digestion measure our right to knowledge. He has it who can use it. As soon as our accumulation overruns our invention or power to use, the evils of intellectual gluttony begin,—congestion of the brain, apoplexy and strangulation.

6. These facts have always suggested to man the sublime creed that the world is not the product of manifold power, but of one will, of one mind; and that one mind is everywhere active, in each ray of the star, in each wavelet of the pool; and whatever opposes that will is everywhere balked and baffled, because things are made so, and not otherwise. Good is positive. Evil is merely privative, not absolute: it is like cold, which is the privation of heat. All evil is so much death or nonentity. Benevolence is absolute and real. So much benevolence as a man hath, so much life hath he. For all things proceed out of this same spirit, which is differently named love, justice, temperance, in its dif-

ferent applications, just as the ocean receives different names on the several shores which it washes.

7. While the immense energy of the sentiment of duty and the awe of the supernatural exert incomparable influence on the mind,— yet it is often perverted, and the tradition received with awe, but without correspondent action of the receiver. Then you find so many men infatuated on that topic! Wise on all other, they lose their head the moment they talk of religion. It is the sturdiest prejudice in the public mind that religion is something by itself; a department distinct from all other experiences, and to which the tests and judgment men are ready enough to show on other things, do not apply. You may sometimes talk with the gravest and best citizen, and the moment the topic of religion is broached, he runs into a childish superstition. His face looks infatuated, and his conversation is. When I talked with an ardent missionary, and pointed out to him that his creed found no support in my experience, he replied, "It is not so in your experience, but is so in the other world." I answer: Other world! there is no other world. God is one and omnipresent; here or nowhere is the whole fact. The one miracle which God works evermore is in Nature, and imparting himself to the mind. When we

ask simply, 'What is true in thought? what is just in action?' it is the yielding of the private heart to the Divine mind, and all personal preferences, and all requiring of wonders, are profane.

8. The conduct of Intellect must respect nothing so much as preserving the sensibility. My measure for all subjects of science as of events is their impression on the soul. That mind is best which is most impressionable. . . . But sensibility does not exhaust our idea of it. That is only half. Genius is not a lazy angel contemplating itself and things. It is insatiable for expression. Thought must take the stupendous step of passing into realization.

The Mind of the Mind

1. The evolution of a highly destined society must be moral; it must run in the grooves of the celestial wheels. It must be catholic in aims. What is *moral?* It is the respecting in action catholic or universal ends. Hear the definition which Kant gives of moral conduct: "Act always so that the immediate motive of thy will may become a universal rule for all intelligent beings."

2. This sentiment lies at the foundation of society, and successively creates all forms of worship. The principle of veneration never dies out. Man fallen into superstition, into sensuality,

is never quite without the visions of the moral sentiment. In like manner, all the expressions of this sentiment are sacred and permanent in proportion to their purity. The expressions of this sentiment affect us more than all other compositions. The sentences of the oldest time, which ejaculate this piety, are still fresh and fragrant. . . . What these holy bards said, all sane men found agreeable and true. And the unique impression of Jesus upon mankind, whose name is not so much written as ploughed into the history of this world, is proof of the subtle virtue of this infusion.

3. The lessons of the moral sentiment are, once for all, an emancipation from that anxiety which takes the joy out of all life. It teaches a great peace. It comes itself from the highest place. It is that, which being in all sound natures, and strongest in the best and most gifted men, we know to be implanted by the Creator of Men. It is a commandment at every moment and in every condition of life to do the duty of that moment and to abstain from doing the wrong. And it is so near and inward and constitutional to each, that no commandment can compare with it in authority. All wise men regard it as the voice of the Creator himself.

4. To a true scholar the attraction of the aspects of nature, the departments of life, and

the passages of his experience, is simply the information they yield him of this supreme nature which lurks within all. That reality, that causing force is moral. The Moral Sentiment is but its other name. It makes by its presence or absence right and wrong, beauty and ugliness, genius or depravation. As the granite comes to the surface and towers into the highest mountains, and, if we dig down, we find it below the superficial strata, so in all the details of our domestic or civil life is hidden the elemental reality, which ever and anon comes to the surface, and forms the grand men, who are the leaders and examples, rather than the companions of the race.

5. For that reality let us stand; that let us serve, and for that speak. Only as far as *that* shines through them are these times or any times worth consideration. I wish to speak of the politics, education, business, and religion around us without ceremony or false deference. You will absolve me from the charge of flippancy, or malignity, or the desire to say smart things at the expense of whomsoever, when you see that reality is all we prize, and that we are bound on our entrance into nature to speak for that.

6. Call it man of honor, or call it Man, the American who would serve his country must learn the beauty and honor of perseverance, he

must reinforce himself by the power of character, and revisit the margin of that well from which his fathers drew waters of life and enthusiasm, the fountain I mean of the moral sentiments, the parent fountain from which this goodly Universe flows as a wave.

7. Out of this fair Idea in the mind springs the effort at the Perfect. It is the interior testimony to a fairer possibility of life and manners which agitates society every day with the offer of some new amendment. If we would make more strict inquiry concerning its origin, we find ourselves rapidly approaching the inner boundaries of thought, that term where speech becomes silence, and science conscience. For the origin of all reform is in that mysterious fountain of the moral sentiment in man, which, amidst the natural, ever contains the supernatural for men. That is new and creative. That is alive. That alone can make a man other than he is. Here or nowhere resides unbounded energy, unbounded power.

8. The intuition of the moral sentiment is an insight of the perfection of the laws of the soul.

9. What is the aboriginal Self, on which a universal reliance may be grounded? What is the nature and power of that science-baffling star, without parallax, without calculable elements, which shoots a ray of beauty even into

trivial and impure actions, if the least mark of independence appear? The inquiry leads us to that source, at once the essence of genius, of virtue, and of life, which we call Spontaneity or Instinct. We denote this primary wisdom as Intuition, whilst all later teachings are tuitions. In that deep force, the last fact behind which analysis cannot go, all things find their common origin.

10. *There is one great source of all special manifestation of spirit. This spirit is self-renewed in each one who will listen, by teachings from within (in-tuitions), and can go out from the receiver to help the world (tuitions),—made clearer by exactly fitting words. This shows the real Self on which men shall rely.**

11. Here is the fountain of action and of thought. Here are the lungs of that inspiration which giveth man wisdom and which cannot be denied without impiety and atheism. We lie in the lap of immense intelligence, which makes us receivers of its truth and organs of its activity. When we discern justice, when we discern truth, we do nothing of ourselves, but allow a passage to its beams. If we ask whence this comes, if we seek to pry into the soul that causes, all philosophy is at fault. Its presence or its absence is

*Emerson's doctrine of intuition, given by Edward Emerson.

all we can affirm. Every man discriminates between the voluntary acts of his mind and his
involuntary perceptions, and knows that to his
involuntary perceptions a perfect faith is due.
He may err in the expression of them, but he
knows that these things are so, like day and
night, not to be disputed.

12. Certain biases, talents, executive skills,
are special to each individual; but the high, con-
templative, all-commanding vision, the sense of
Right and Wrong, is alike in all. Its attributes
are self-existence, eternity, intuition and command. It is the mind of the mind. We belong to
it, not it to us. It is in all men, and constitutes
them men. In bad men it is dormant, as health is
in men entranced or drunken; but, however in-
operative, it exists underneath whatever vices
and errors. The extreme simplicity of this intuition embarrasses every attempt at analysis. We
can only mark, one by one, the perfections which
it combines in every act. It admits of no appeal,
looks to no superior essence. It is the reason of
things.

13. Whosoever looks with heed into his
thoughts will find that our science of the mind
has not got far. He will find there is somebody
within him that knows more than he does, a certain dumb life in life; a simple wisdom behind
all acquired wisdom; somewhat not educated or

educable; not altered or alterable; a mother-wit which does not learn by experience or by books, but knew it all already; makes no progress, but was wise in youth as in age. More or less clouded it yet resides the same in all, saying *Ay, ay,* or *No, no,* to every proposition. Yet its grand *Ay* and its grand *No* are more musical than all eloquence. Nobody has found the limit of its knowledge. Whatever object is brought before it is already well known to it. Its justice is perfect; its look is catholic and universal, its light ubiquitous like the sun. It does not put forth organs, it rests in presence: yet trusted and obeyed in happy natures it becomes active and salient, and makes new means for its great ends.

14. Meantime, whilst the doors of the temple stand open, night and day, before every man, and the oracles of this truth cease never, it is guarded by one stern condition; this, namely: it is an intuition. It cannot be received at second hand. Truly speaking, it is not instruction, but provocation, that I can receive from another soul. What he announces, I must find true in me, or reject; and on his word, or as his second, be he who he may, I can accept nothing. On the contrary, the absence of this primary faith is the presence of degradation. As is the flood, so is the ebb. Let this faith depart, and the very words it spake and the things it made become false

and hurtful. Then falls the church, the state, art, letters, life. The doctrine of the divine nature being forgotten, a sickness infects and dwarfs the constitution. Once man was all; now he is an appendage, a nuisance. And because the indwelling Supreme Spirit cannot wholly be got rid of, the doctrine of it suffers this perversion, that the divine nature is attributed to one or two persons, and denied to all the rest, and denied with fury. The doctrine of inspiration is lost; the base doctrine of the majority of voices usurps the place of the doctrine of the soul. Miracles, prophecy, poetry, the ideal life, the holy life, exist as ancient history merely; they are not in the belief, nor in the aspiration of society; but, when suggested, seem ridiculous. Life is comic or pitiful as soon as the high ends of being fade out of sight, and man becomes near-sighted, and can only attend to what addresses the senses.

The Mid-World

1. Human strength is not in extremes, but in avoiding extremes.

2. Of what use is genius, if the organ is too convex or too concave and cannot find a focal distance within the actual horizon of human life? Of what use, if the brain is too cold or too hot, and the man does not care enough for results to stimulate him to experiment, and hold him up in it? or if the web is too finely woven, too irritable by pleasure and pain, so that life stagnates from too much reception without due outlet?

3. Our love of the real draws us to perma-

nence, but health of body consists in circulation, and sanity of mind in variety or facility of association. We need change of objects. Dedication to one thought is quickly odious.

4. Life itself is a mixture of power and form, and will not bear the least excess of either. To finish the moment, to find the journey's end in every step of the road, to live the greatest number of good hours, is wisdom.

5. Without any shadow of doubt, amidst this vertigo of shows and politics, I settle myself ever the firmer in the creed that we should not postpone and refer and wish, but do broad justice where we are, by whomsoever we deal with, accepting our actual companions and circumstances, however humble or odious, as the mystic officials to whom the universe has delegated its whole pleasure for us.

6. The middle region of our being is the temperate zone. We may climb into the thin and cold realm of pure geometry and lifeless science, or sink into that of sensation. Between these extremes is the equator of life, of thought, of spirit, of poetry,—a narrow belt.

7. The mid-world is best.

8. Undulation, alternation is the condition of progress, of life.

9. Solitude is naught and society is naught. Alternate them and the good of each is seen.

10. If you do not quit the high chair, lie quite down, and roll on the ground a good deal, you become nervous and heavy-hearted.

11. The dog that was fed on sugar died.

12. Do not craze yourself with thinking, but go about your business anywhere. Life is not intellectual or critical, but sturdy. Its chief good is for well-mixed people who can enjoy what they find, without question. . . . To fill the hour, —that is happiness; to fill the hour and leave no crevice for a repentance or an approval.

13. The practical aim is forever higher than the literary aim.

14. I have no quarrel with action, only I prefer no action to misaction, and I reject the abusive application of the term *practical* to those lower activities.

15. *Save on the low levels and spend on the high levels. That is forever practical.*

16. *Face life as it really is. That is forever practical.*

17. We feel as the minister about the Cape Cod farm,—in the old time when the minister was still invited, in the spring, to make a prayer for the blessing of a piece of land,—the good pastor being brought to the spot, stopped short: "No, this land does not want a prayer, this land wants manure."

18. And evermore in the world is this

marvellous balance of beauty and disgust, magnificence and rats.

19. There are all degrees of proficiency in knowledge of the world. It is sufficient to our present purpose to indicate three. One class live to the utility of the symbol, esteeming health and wealth a final good. Another class live above this mark to the beauty of the symbol, as the poet and artist and the naturalist and man of science. A third class live above the beauty of the symbol to the beauty of the thing signified; these are wise men. The first class have common sense; the second, taste; and the third, spiritual perception. Once in a long time, a man traverses the whole scale, and sees and enjoys the symbol solidly, then also has a clear eye for its beauty, and lastly, whilst he pitches his tent on this sacred volcanic isle of nature, does not offer to build houses and barns thereon,—reverencing the splendor of the God which he sees bursting through each chink and cranny.

20. Man Thinking . . . should occupy the whole space between God or pure mind and the multitude of uneducated men. He must draw from the infinite Reason, on one side; and he must penetrate into the heart and sense of the crowd, on the other. From one, he must draw his strength; to the other, he must owe his aim. The one yokes him to the real; the other, to the

apparent. At one pole is Reason; at the other, Common Sense. If he be defective at either extreme of the scale, his philosophy will seem low and utilitarian, or it will appear too vague and indefinite for the uses of life.

21. Youthful aspirations are fine things, your theories and plans of life are fair and commendable:—but will you stick?

22. The hero is he who is immovably centred. The main difference between people seems to be that one man can come under obligations on which you can rely,—is obligable; and another is not. As he has not a law within him, there's nothing to tie him to.

23. All rests at last on that integrity which dwarfs talent, and can spare it. Sanity consists in not being subdued by your means.

24. All our progress is an unfolding, like the vegetable bud. You have first an instinct, then an opinion, then a knowledge, as the plant has root, bud and fruit. Trust the instinct to the end, though you can render no reason. It is vain to hurry it. By trusting it to the end, it shall ripen into truth and you shall know why you believe. . . .

This instinctive action never ceases in a healthy mind, but becomes richer and more frequent in its informations through all states of culture.

25. I will trust my instincts. For always a reason halts after an instinct, and when I have deviated from the instinct, comes somebody with a profound theory teaching that I ought to have followed it: some Goethe, Swedenborg, or Carlyle.

26. Do not be too timid and squeamish about your actions. All life is an experiment. The more experiments you make the better. What if they are a little coarse, and you may get your coat soiled or torn? What if you do fail, and get fairly rolled in the dirt once or twice? Up again you shall never be so afraid of a tumble.

27. We are very apt to over-rate the importance of our actions. . . . The true way to consider things is this: Truth says, Give yourself no manner of anxiety about events, about the consequences of actions . . . The whole object of the universe to us is the formation of character. If you think you came into being for the purpose of taking an important part in the administration of events, to guard a province of the moral creation from ruin, and that its salvation hangs on the success of your single arm, you have wholly mistaken your business.

28. The secret of culture is to learn that a few great points steadily reappear, alike in the poverty of the obscurest farm and in the mis-

cellany of metropolitan life, and that these few are alone to be regarded;—the escape from all false ties; courage to be what we are, and love of what is simple and beautiful; independence and cheerful relation, these are the essentials, —these, and the wish to serve, to add somewhat to the well-being of men.

The Life of the Spirit

1. The true meaning of *spiritual* is *real;* that law which executes itself, which works without means, and which cannot be conceived as not existing.

2. I can best indicate by examples those reactions by which every part of nature replies to the purpose of the actor,—beneficently to the good, penally to the bad. Let us replace sentimentalism by realism, and dare to uncover those simple and terrible laws which, be they seen or unseen, pervade and govern.

3. The spirit only can teach. Not any profane man, not any sensual, not any liar, not any

slave can teach, but only he can give, who has; he only can create, who is. The man on whom the soul descends, through whom the soul speaks, alone can teach. Courage, piety, love, wisdom, can teach; and every man can open his door to these angels, and they shall bring him the gift of tongues. But the man who aims to speak as books enable, as synods use, as the fashion guides, and as interest commands, babbles. Let him hush.

4. Every mind must know the whole lesson for itself, must go over the whole ground. What it does not see, what it does not live, it will not know.

5. I believe in the existence of the material world as the expression of the spiritual or the real, and in the impenetrable mystery which hides (and hides through absolute transparency) the mental nature, I await the insight which our advancing knowledge of material laws shall furnish.

6. Once men thought Spirit divine, and Matter diabolic; one Ormuzd, the other Ahriman. Now science and philosophy recognize the parallelism, the approximation, the unity of the two: how each reflects the other as face answers to face in a glass: nay, how the laws of both are one, or how one is the realization. We are learning not to fear truth.

7. Man is conscious of a universal soul within or behind his individual life, wherein, as in a firmament, the natures of Justice, Truth, Love, Freedom, arise and shine. This universal soul he calls Reason: it is not mine, or thine, or his, but we are its; we are its property and men.

8. That which intellectually considered we call Reason, considered in relation to nature, we call Spirit. Spirit is the Creator. Spirit hath life in itself. And man in all ages and countries embodies it in his language as the FATHER.

9. The world proceeds from the same spirit as the body of man. It is a remoter and inferior incarnation of God, a projection of God in the unconscious. But it differs from the body in one important respect. It is not, like that, now subjected to the human will. Its serene order is inviolable by us. It is, therefore, to us, the present expositor of the divine mind. It is a fixed point whereby we may measure our departure. As we degenerate, the contrast between us and our house is more evident. We are as much strangers in nature as we are aliens from God.

10. It is a low benefit to give me something; it is a high benefit to enable me to do somewhat of myself. The time is coming when all men will see that the gift of God to the soul is not a vaunting, overpowering, excluding sanc-

tity, but a sweet, natural goodness, a goodness like thine and mine, and that so invites thine and mine to be and to grow.

11. To Be is the unsolved, unsolvable wonder. To Be, in its two connections of inward and outward, the mind and Nature. The wonder subsists, and age, though of eternity, could not approach a solution. But the suggestion is always returning, that hidden source publishing at once our being and that it is the source of outward Nature. Who are we, and what is Nature, have one answer in the life that rushes into us.

12. Our eating, trading, marrying, and learning are mistaken by us for ends and realities, whilst they are properly symbols only; when we have come, by a divine leading, into the inner firmament, we are apprised of the unreality or representative character of what we esteemed final.

13. All things proceed out of the same spirit, and all things conspire with it. Whilst a man seeks good ends, he is strong by the whole strength of nature. In so far as he roves from these ends, he bereaves himself of power, or auxiliaries; his being shrinks out of all remote channels, he becomes less and less, a mote, a point, until absolute badness is absolute death.

14. The perception of this law of laws

awakens in the mind a sentiment which we call the religious sentiment, and which makes our highest happiness. Wonderful is its power to charm and to command. It is a mountain air.

15. This sentiment is divine and deifying. It is the beatitude of man. It makes him illimitable. Through it, the soul first knows itself. It corrects the capital mistake of the infant man, who seeks to be great by following the great, and hopes to derive advantages *from another,* —by showing the fountain of all good to be in himself, and that he, equally with every man, is an inlet into the deeps of Reason. When he says, "I ought"; when love warms him; when he chooses, warned from on high, the good and great deed; then, deep melodies wander through his soul from Supreme Wisdom.—Then he can worship, and be enlarged by his worship; for he can never go behind this sentiment. In the sublimest flights of the soul, rectitude is never surmounted, love is never outgrown.

16. We shall pass for what we are. Do not fear to die because you have not done your task. Whenever a noble soul comes, the audience awaits. And he is not judged by his performance, but by the spirit of his performance. . . .

17. Certainly I go for culture, and not for multitudes. . . .

18. Be an opener of doors for such as come

after thee, and do not try to make the universe a blind alley.

19. Nature forever puts a premium on reality. What is done for effect is seen to be done for effect; what is done for love is felt to be done for love. A man inspires affection and honor because he was not lying in wait for these. The things of a man for which we visit him were done in the dark and the cold. A little integrity is better than any career.

20. The youth puts off the illusions of the child, the man puts off the ignorance and tumultuous passions of youth; proceeding thence puts off the egotism of manhood, and becomes at last a public and universal soul. He is rising to greater heights, but also rising to realities; the outer relations and circumstances dying out, he entering deeper into God, God into him, until the last garment of egotism falls, and he is with God,—shares the will and the immensity of the First Cause.

High Levels

1. The foregoing generations beheld God and nature face to face; we, through their eyes. Why should not we also enjoy an original relation to the universe? Why should not we have a poetry and philosophy of insight and not of tradition, and a religion by revelation to us, and not the history of theirs?

2. The day of days, the great day of the feast of life, is that in which the inward eye opens to the Unity in things, to the omnipresence of law:—sees that what is must be and ought to be, or is the best. This beatitude dips from on high down on us and we see. It is not

in us so much as we are in it. If the air come to
our lungs, we breathe and live; if not, we die.
If the light come to our eyes, we see; else not.
And if truth come to our mind we suddenly
expand to its dimensions, as if we grew to
worlds. We are as lawgivers; we speak for
Nature; we prophesy and divine.

3. This insight, which expresses itself by
what is called Imagination, is a very high sort
of seeing, which does not come by study, but by
the intellect being where and what it sees; by
sharing the path or circuit of things through
forms, and so making them translucid to others.

4. This insight throws us on the party and
interest of the Universe, against all and sundry;
against ourselves as much as others. A man
speaking from insight affirms of himself what is
true of the mind: seeing its immortality, he
says, I am immortal; seeing its invincibility, he
says, I am strong. It is not in us, but we are in
it. It is of the maker, not of what is made. All
things are touched and changed by it. This uses
and is not used. It distances those who share it
from those who share it not. Those who share
it not are flocks and herds. It dates from itself;
not from former men or better men, gospel, or
constitution, or college, or custom.

5. The intuition of the moral sentiment is
an insight of the perfection of the laws of the

soul. These laws execute themselves. They are out of time, out of space, and not subject to circumstance. Thus in the soul of man there is a justice whose retributions are instant and entire. He who does a good deed is instantly ennobled. He who does a mean deed is by the action itself contracted. He who puts off impurity, thereby puts on purity. If a man is at heart just, then in so far is he God; the safety of God, the immortality of God, the majesty of God do enter into that man with justice. If a man dissemble, deceive, he deceives himself, and goes out of acquaintance with his own being. A man in the view of absolute goodness, adores, with total humility. Every step so downward, is a step upward. The man who renounces himself, comes to himself.

6. It is a secret which every intellectual man quickly learns, that beyond the energy of his possessed and conscious intellect he is capable of a new energy (as of an intellect doubled on itself), by abandonment to the nature of things; that beside his privacy of power as an individual man, there is a great public power on which he can draw, by unlocking, at all risks, his human doors, and suffering the ethereal tides to roll and circulate through him; then he is caught up into the life of the Universe, his speech is thunder, his

thought is law, and his words are universally intelligible. . . .

7. It is certain that worship stands in some commanding relation to the health of man and to his highest powers, so as to be in some manner the source of intellect. All the great ages have been ages of belief. I mean, when there was any extraordinary power of performance, when great national movements began, when arts appeared, when heroes existed, when poems were made,—the human soul was in earnest, and had fixed its thoughts on spiritual verities with as strict a grasp as that of the hands on the sword, or the pencil, or the trowel. It is true that genius takes its rise out of the mountains of rectitude; that all beauty and power which men covet are somehow born out of that Alpine district; that any extraordinary degree of beauty in man or woman involves a moral charm. Thus I think we very slowly admit in another man a higher degree of moral sentiment than our own,—a finer conscience, more impressionable or which marks minuter degrees; an ear to hear acuter notes of right and wrong than we can. I think we listen suspiciously and very slowly to any evidence to that point. But, once satisfied of such superiority, we set no limit to our expectation of his genius. For such persons are nearer to the secret of God than others; are

bathed by sweeter waters; they hear notices, they see visions, where others are vacant. We believe that holiness confers a certain insight, because not by our private but by our public force can we share and know the nature of things.

8. A deep insight will always, like Nature, ultimate its thought in a thing. As soon as a man masters a principle and sees his facts in relation to it, fields, waters, skies, offer to clothe his thoughts in images. Then all men understand him; Parthian, Mede, Chinese, Spaniard and Indian hear their own tongue. For he can now find symbols of universal significance, which are readily rendered into any dialect; as a painter, a sculptor, a musician, can in their several ways express the same sentiment of anger, or love, or religion.

9. The height of culture, the highest behavior, consists in the identification of the Ego with the universe; so that when a man says I hope, I find, I think, he might properly say, The human race thinks or finds or hopes. And meantime he shall be able continually to keep sight of his biographical Ego,—I have a desk, I have an office, I am hungry, I had an ague,— as rhetoric or offset to his grand spiritual Ego, without impertinence, or ever confounding them.

I may well say this is divine, the continuation of the divine effort. Alas! it seems not to be ours, to be quite independent of us. Often there is so little affinity between the man and his works that we think the wind must have writ them. Also its communication from one to another follows its own law and refuses our intrusion.

10. The superiority of the man is in the simplicity of his thought, that he has no obstruction, but looks straight at the pure fact, with no color of option. Profound sincerity is the only basis . . . of character. The virtue of the Intellect is its own, its courage is of its own kind, and at last it will be justified, though for the moment it seem hostile to what it most reveres.

11. Moreover, because Nature is moral, that mind only can see, in which the same order entirely obtains. An interchangeable Truth, Beauty and Goodness, each wholly interfused in the other, must make the humors of that eye which would see causes reaching to their last effect and reproducing the world forever.

12. This necessity of resting on the real, of speaking *your* private thought and experience, few young men apprehend. . . . Let that belief which you hold alone, have free course. I have observed that in all public speaking, the

rule of the orator begins, not in the array of his facts, but when his deep conviction, and the right and necessity he feels to convey that conviction to his audience,—when these shine and burn in his address; when the thought which he stands for gives its own authority to him, adds to him a grander personality, gives him valor, breadth and new intellectual power, so that not he, but mankind, seems to speak through his lips.

13. Nothing is more simple than greatness; indeed, to be simple is to be great. The vision of genius comes by renouncing the too officious activity of the understanding, and giving leave and amplest privilege to the spontaneous sentiment. Out of this must all that is alive and genial in thought go. Men grind and grind in the mill of a truism, and nothing comes out but what was put in. But the moment they desert the tradition for a spontaneous thought, then poetry, wit, hope, virtue, learning, anecdote, all flock to their aid.

14. And what is Genius but finer love, a love impersonal, a love of the flower and perfection of things, and a desire to draw a new picture or copy of the same? It looks to the cause and life: it proceeds from within outward, whilst Talent goes from without inward. Talent finds its models, methods and ends, in society,

exists for exhibition, and goes to the soul only
for power to work. Genius is its own end, and
draws its means and the style of its architecture
from within, going abroad only for audience
and spectator, as we adapt our voice and phrase
to the distance and character of the ear we
speak to.

15. Genius is the naturalist or geographer
of the supersensible regions, and draws their
map; and, by acquainting us with new fields
of activity, cools our affection for the old. These
are at once accepted as the reality, of which the
world we have conversed with is the show.

16. Thou must mount for love
     Into vision where all form
     In one only form dissolves.

     Pray for a beam
     Out of that sphere,
     Thee to guide and to redeem.

17. He that feeds men serveth few;
     He serves all who dares be true.

18. Heartily know,
     When half-gods go,
     The gods arrive.

19. Throb thine with Nature's throbbing
         breast,
     And all is clear from east to west.

The Law of Laws

1. Is not the law of compensation perfect? It holds as far as we can see. Different gifts to different individuals, but with a mortgage of responsibility on every one. 'The gods *sell* all things.'

2. Let me embark in political economy, in repartee, in fiction, in verse, in practical counsels . . . and I am soon run aground; but let my bark head its own way toward the law of laws, toward the compensation or action and reaction of the moral universe, and I sweep serenely over God's depths in an infinite sea.

3. You hold up your pasteboard religion for the people who are unfit for a true. So you

say. But presently there will arise a race of preachers who will take such hold of the omnipotence of truth that they will blow the old falsehood to shreds with the breath of their mouth. There is no material show so splendid, no poem so musical as the great law of Compensation in our moral nature. When an ardent mind once gets a glimpse of that perfect beauty, and sees how it envelopes him and determines all his being, will he easily slide back to a periodic shouting about 'blood atoning'? I apprehend that the religious history of society is to show a pretty rapid abandonment of forms of worship and the renovation and exaltation of preaching into real anxious instruction.

4. The whole of what we know is a system of compensations.

5. Ever since I was a boy I have wished to write a discourse on Compensation; for it seemed to me when very young that on this subject life was ahead of theology and the people knew more than the preachers taught.

6. It seemed to me also that in it might be shown men a ray of divinity, the present action of the soul of this world, clean from all vestige of tradition; and so the heart of man might be bathed by an inundation of eternal love, conversing with that which he knows was always and always must be, because it really is now.

It appeared moreover that if this doctrine could be stated in terms with any resemblance to those bright intuitions in which this truth is sometimes revealed to us, it would be a star in many dark hours and crooked passages in our journey, that would not suffer us to lose our way.

7. Polarity, or action and reaction, we meet in every part of nature; in darkness and light; in heat and cold; in the ebb and flow of waters; in male and female; in the inspiration and expiration of plants and animals; in the equation of quantity and quality in the fluids of the animal body; in the systole and diastole of the heart; in the undulations of fluids and of sound; in the centrifugal and centripetal gravity; in electricity, galvanism, and chemical affinity. Superinduce magnetism at one end of a needle, the opposite magnetism takes place at the other end. If the south attracts, the north repels. To empty here, you must condense there. An inevitable dualism bisects nature, so that each thing is a half, and suggests another thing to make it whole; as, spirit, matter; man, woman; odd, even; subjective, objective; in, out; upper, under; motion, rest; yea, nay.

8. Whilst the world is thus dual, so is every one of its parts. The entire system of things gets represented in every particle.

9. The same dualism underlies the nature

and condition of man. Every excess causes a defect; every defect an excess. Every sweet hath its
sour; every evil its good. Every faculty which is
a receiver of pleasure has an equal penalty put
on its abuse. It is to answer for its moderation
with its life. For every grain of wit there is a
grain of folly. For every thing you have missed,
you have gained something else; and for every
thing you gain, you lose something. If riches in-
crease, they are increased that use them. If the
gatherer gathers too much, Nature takes out of
the man what she puts into his chest; swells the
estate, but kills the owner.

10.   These appearances indicate the fact that
the universe is represented in every one of its
particles. Every thing in nature contains all the
powers of nature. Every thing is made of one
hidden stuff. . . .

11.   The value of the universe contrives to
throw itself into every point. If the good is
there, so is the evil; if the affinity, so the re-
pulsion; if the force, so the limitation.

12.   Thus is the universe alive. All things
are moral. That soul which within us is a sentiment, outside of us is a law. We feel its inspiration; but there in history we can see its
fatal strength. "It is in the world, and the world
was made by it." Justice is not postponed. A
perfect equity adjusts its balance in all parts of

life . . . The dice of God are always loaded.

13. Every secret is told, every crime is punished, every virtue rewarded, every wrong redressed, in silence and certainty. What we call retribution is the universal necessity by which the whole appears wherever a part appears.

14. Every act rewards itself, or in other words integrates itself, in a twofold manner; first in the thing, or in real nature; and secondly in the circumstance, or in apparent nature. Men call the circumstance the retribution. The causal retribution is in the thing and is seen by the soul. The retribution in the circumstance is seen by the understanding; it is inseparable from the thing, but is often spread over a long time and so does not become distinct until after many years. The specific stripes may follow late after the offence, but they follow because they accompany it. Crime and punishment grow out of one stem. Punishment is a fruit that unsuspected ripens within the flower of the pleasure which concealed it. Cause and effect, means and ends, seed and fruit, cannot be severed; for the effect already blooms in the cause, the end pre-exists in the means, the fruit in the seed.

15. The parted water reunites behind our hand. Pleasure is taken out of pleasant things, profit out of profitable things, power out of

strong things, as soon as we seek to separate them from the whole. We can no more halve things and get the sensual good, by itself, than we can get an inside that shall have no outside, or a light without a shadow.

16. What will you have? quoth God; pay for it and take it.—Nothing venture, nothing have.—Thou shalt be paid exactly for what thou hast done, no more, no less.

17. It is thus written, because it is thus in life. Our action is overmastered and character-ized above our will by the law of nature. We aim at a petty end quite aside from the public good, but our act arranges itself by irresistible magnetism in a line with the poles of the world.

18. A man cannot speak but he judges himself. With his will or against his will he draws his portrait to the eye of his companions by every word. Every opinion reacts on him who utters it.

19. There is a deeper fact in the soul than compensation, to wit, its own nature. The soul is not a compensation, but a life. The soul *is.* Under all this running sea of circumstance, whose waters ebb and flow with perfect bal-ance, lies the aboriginal abyss of real Being. Essence, or God, is not a relation or a part, but the whole. Being is the vast affirmative, exclud-ing negation, self-balanced, and swallowing up

all relations, parts and times within itself. Nature, truth, virtue, are the influx from thence. Vice is the absence or departure of the same.

20. So use all that is called Fortune. Most men gamble with her, and gain all, and lose all, as her wheel rolls. But do thou leave as unlawful these winnings, and deal with Cause and Effect, the chancellors of God. In the Will work and acquire, and thou hast chained the wheel of Chance, and shall sit hereafter out of fear from her rotations. A political victory, a rise of rents, the recovery of your sick or the return of your absent friend, or some other favorable event raises your spirits, and you think good days are preparing for you. Do not believe it. Nothing can bring you peace but yourself. Nothing can bring you peace but the triumph of principles.

21. Skepticism is unbelief in cause and effect. A man does not see that as he eats, so he thinks; as he deals, so he is, and so he appears . . . As we are, so we do; and as we do, so is it done to us; we are the builders of our fortunes; cant and lying and the attempt to secure a good which does not belong to us, are, once for all, balked and vain. But, in the human mind, this tie of fate is made alive. The law is the basis of the human mind. In us, it is inspiration; out there in nature we see its fatal strength. We call it the moral sentiment.

22. Nature punishes any neglect of prudence. If you think the senses final, obey their law. If you believe in the soul, do not clutch at sensual sweetness before it is ripe on the slow tree of cause and effect.

23. Everything lasts in proportion to its beauty. In proportion as it was not polluted by the wilfulness of the writer, but flowed from his mind after the divine order of cause and effect, it was not his, but Nature's, and shared the sublimity of the sea and sky.

24. Truth, or the connection between cause and effect, alone interests us. We are persuaded that a thread runs through all things: all worlds are strung on it, as beads; and men, and events, and life, come to us only because of that thread: they pass and repass only that we may know the direction and continuity of that line. . . . Talent makes counterfeit ties; genius finds the real ones.

25. The Teacher that I look for and await shall enunciate with more precision and universality, with piercing poetic insight those beautiful yet severe compensations that give to moral nature an aspect of mathematical science. He will not occupy himself in laboriously reanimating a historical religion, but in bringing men to God by showing them that he is, not was, and speaks, not spoke.

The Universal Outlook

1. You are rightly fond of certain books or men that you have found to excite your reverence and emulation. But none of these can compare with the greatness of that counsel which is open to you in happy solitude. I mean that there is for you the following of an inward leader,—a slow discrimination that there is for each a Best Counsel which enjoins the fit word and the fit act for every moment. And the path of each, pursued, leads to greatness. How grateful to find in man or woman a new emphasis of their own.

2. The man of this age must be matricu-

lated in the university of sciences and tendencies flowing from all past periods. He must not be one who can be surprised and shipwrecked by every bold or subtile word which malignant and acute men may utter in his hearing, but should be taught all skepticisms and unbeliefs, and made the destroyer of all card-houses and paper walls, and the sifter of all opinions, by being put face to face from his infancy with Reality.

3. There is not a piece of science but its flank may be turned to-morrow; there is not any literary reputation, not the so-called eternal names of fame, that may not be revised and condemned. The very hopes of man, the thoughts of his heart, the religion of nations, the manners and morals of mankind are all at the mercy of a new generalization.

4. The soul knows no persons. It invites every man to expand to the full circle of the universe, and will have no preferences but those of spontaneous love.

5. O father, O mother, O wife, O brother, O friend, I have lived with you after appearances hitherto. Henceforward I am the truth's. Be it known unto you that henceforward I obey no law less than the eternal law. I will have no covenants but proximities. I shall endeavor to nourish my parents, to support my family, to be

the chaste husband of one wife,—but these relations I must fill after a new and unprecedented way. I appeal from your customs. I must be myself. I cannot break myself any longer for you, or you. If you can love me for what I am, we shall be the happier. If you cannot, I will still seek to deserve that you should. I will not hide my tastes or aversions. I will so trust that what is deep is holy, that I will do strongly before the sun and moon whatever inly rejoices me and the heart appoints. If you are noble, I will love you; if you are not, I will not hurt you and myself by hypocritical attentions. If you are true, but not in the same truth with me, cleave to your companions; I will seek my own. I do this not selfishly but humbly and truly. It is alike your interest, and mine, and all men's, however long we have dwelt in lies, to live in truth. Does this sound harsh today? You will soon love what is dictated by your nature as well as mine, and if we follow the truth it will bring us out safe at last.

6. If we should ask ourselves what is this self-respect, it would carry us to the highest problems. It is our practical perception of the Deity in man. It has its deep foundations in religion. If you have ever known a good mind among the Quakers, you will have found *that* is the element of their faith. As they express it,

it might be thus: "I do not pretend to any commandment or large revelation, but if at any
time I form some plan, propose a journey or a
course of conduct, I perhaps find a silent ob-
stacle in my mind that I cannot account for.
Very well,—I let it lie, thinking it may pass
away, but if it do not pass away I yield to it,
obey it. You ask me to describe it. I cannot
describe it. It is not an oracle, nor an angel, nor
a dream, nor a law; it is too simple to be described, it is but a grain of mustard-seed, but
such as it is, it is something which the contra-
diction of all mankind could not shake, and
which the consent of all mankind could not con-
firm."

7. Man is endogenous, and education is his
unfolding. . . . Right ethics are central and go
from the soul outward. Gift is contrary to the
law of the universe. Serving others is serving
us. I must absolve me to myself. 'Mind thy
affair,' says the spirit:—'coxcomb, would you
meddle with the skies, or with other people?'

8. God delights to isolate us every day, and
hide from us the past and the future. . . . 'You
will not remember,' he seems to say, 'and you
will not expect.' All good conversation, manners and action come from a spontaneity which
forgets usages and makes the moment great.

9. The consciousness in each man is a slid-

ing scale, which identifies him now with the First Cause, and now with the flesh of his body; life above life, in infinite degrees. The sentiment from which it sprung determines the dignity of any deed, and the question ever is, not what you have done or forborne, but at whose command you have done or forborne it.

10. Man's life is a progress, and not a station.

11. The wise man shows his wisdom in separation, in gradation, and his scale of creatures and of merits is as wide as nature. The foolish have no range in their scale. . . .

12. A man cannot utter two or three sentences without disclosing to intelligent ears precisely where he stands in life and thought, namely, whether in the kingdom of the senses . . . or in that of ideas . . . or in the realm of intuitions . . . People seem not to see that their opinion of the world is also a confession of character. We can only see what we are . . .

13. A wise man will never impawn his future being and action, and decide beforehand what he shall do in a given extreme event. Nature and God will instruct him in that hour.

14. If the first rule [of progress] is to obey your genius, in the second place the good mind is known by the choice of what is positive, of what is advancing. We must embrace the affir-

mative . . . Strength enters as the moral element enters . . . Good will makes insight.

15. But if instead of these negatives you give me affirmatives; if you tell me that there is always life for the living; that what man has done man can do; that this world belongs to the energetic; that there is always a way to everything desirable; that every man is provided, in the new bias of his faculty, with a key to Nature, and that man only rightly knows himself as far as he has experimented on things, —I am invigorated, put into genial and working temper; the horizon opens . . .

16. Why drag about this corpse of your memory, lest you contradict somewhat you have stated in this or that public place? Suppose you should contradict yourself; what then? It seems to be a rule of wisdom never to rely on your memory alone, scarcely even in acts of pure memory, but to bring the past for judgment into the thousand-eyed present, and live ever in a new day.

17. The mind goes antagonizing on, and never prospers but by fits. We thrive by casualties. . . . Every man is an impossibility until he is born, every thing impossible until we see it a success.

18. Nations die by suicide. The sign of it is the decay of thought.

19. The way to mend the bad world is to create the right world.

20. Wealth is mental; wealth is moral. . . . a dollar goes on increasing in value with all the genius and all the virtue in the world.

21. That repose which is the ornament and ripeness of man is not American. That repose which indicates a faith in the laws of the universe,—a faith that they will fulfil themselves, and are not to be impeded, transgressed or accelerated. Our people are too slight and vain. They are easily elated and easily depressed. . . . Our people act on the moment, and from external impulse. They all lean on some other, and this superstitiously, and not from insight of his merit. They follow a fact; they follow success, and not skill. . . . Therefore, as soon as the success stops and the admirable man blunders, they quit him; already they remember that they long ago suspected his judgment, and they transfer the repute of judgment to the next prosperous person who has not yet blundered. Of course this levity makes them as easily despond.

22. "There are two things," said Mahomet, "which I abhor, the learned in his infidelities, and the fool in his devotions." Our times are impatient of both, and specially of the last. Let us have nothing now which is not its own

evidence. There is surely enough for the heart and imagination in the religion itself. Let us not be pestered with assertions and half-truths, with emotion and snuffle.

23. The natural remedy against this miscellany of knowledge and aim, this desultory universality of ours, is to substitute realism for sentimentalism; a certain recognition of the simple and terrible laws which, seen or unseen, pervade and govern.

24. God offers to every mind its choice between truth and repose. Take which you please,—you can never have both. Between these, as a pendulum, man oscillates. He in whom the love of repose predominates will accept the first creed, the first philosophy, the first political party he meets,—most likely his father's. He gets rest, commodity and reputation; but he shuts the door of truth. He in whom the love of truth predominates will keep himself aloof from all moorings, and afloat. He will abstain from dogmatism, and recognize all the opposite negations between which, as walls, his being is swung. He submits to the inconvenience of suspense and imperfect opinion, but he is a candidate for truth, as the other is not, and respects the highest law of his being.

25. *That repose which is the ornament and ripeness of man is not the repose which accepts*

the first creed, the first philosophy, the first political party it meets. One is the serenity born of understanding, while the latter is the inertia born of spiritual dullness.

26. Without the rich heart, wealth is an ugly beggar.

27. Life is a train of moods like a string of beads, and as we pass through them they prove to be many-colored lenses which paint the world their own hue, and each shows only what lies in its focus. From the mountain you see the mountain. We animate what we can, and we see only what we animate.

28. Let us drop this idolatry. Let us give over this mendicancy. Let us even bid our dearest friends farewell, and defy them, saying 'Who are you? Unhand me: I will be dependent no more.' Ah! seest thou not, O brother, that thus we part only to meet again on a higher platform, and only be more each other's because we are more our own?

29. We must be our own before we can be another's.

30. Thus even love, which is the deification of persons, must become more impersonal every day.

31. He is a new man, with new perceptions, new and keener purposes, and a religious solemnity of character and aims. He does not

longer appertain to his family and society; *he* is somewhat; *he* is a person; *he* is a soul.

32. Let our affection flow out to our fellows; it would operate in a day the greatest of all revolutions. It is better to work on institutions by the sun than by the wind.

33. It is of little consequence in what manner, through what organs . . . holiness is effected. . . . The mind, once prepared for the reign of principles, will easily find modes of expressing its will.

34. Nature has a higher end, in the production of new individuals, than security, namely *ascension,* or the passage of the soul into higher forms.

35. The only sin is limitation.

36. The *first* Philosophy, that of mind, is the science of what *is,* in distinction from what *appears.* It is one mark of its laws that their enunciation awakens the feeling of the moral sublime, and *great men* are they who believe in them.

Truth

1. Truth is simple, and will not be antique; is ever present and insists on being of this age and of this moment. Here is thought and love and truth and duty, new as on the first day of Adam and of angels.

2. The one condition coupled with the gift of truth is its use.

3. One may say boldly that no man has a right perception of any truth who has not been reacted on by it so as to be ready to be its martyr.

4. The truth is in the air, and the most impressionable brain will announce it first, but

all will announce it a few minutes later. So
women, as most susceptible, are the best index
of the coming hour. So the great man, that is,
the man most imbued with the spirit of the time,
is the impressionable man;—of a fibre irritable
and delicate, like iodine to light. He feels the
infinitesimal attractions. His mind is righter
than others because he yields to a current so
feeble as can be felt only by a needle delicately
poised.

5. The senses minister to a mind they do
not know. At a moment in our history the mind's
eye opens and we become aware of spiritual
facts, of rights, of duties, of thoughts,—a thousand faces of one essence. We call the essence
Truth; the particular aspects of it we call
thoughts. These facts, this essence, are not new;
they are old and eternal, but our seeing of them
is new. Having seen them we are no longer
brute lumps whirled by Fate, but we pass into
the council-chamber and government of Nature.
In so far as we see them we share their life and
sovereignty.

6. It is the office, I doubt not, of this age
to annul that adulterous divorce which the superstition of many ages has effected between the
intellect and holiness. The lovers of goodness
have been one class, the students of wisdom another; as if either could exist in any purity with-

out the other. Truth is always holy, holiness always wise. I will that we keep terms with sin and a sinful literature and society no longer, but live a life of discovery and performance.

7. There is a certain wisdom of humanity which is common to the greatest men with the lowest, and which our ordinary education often labors to silence and obstruct. The mind is one, and the best minds, who love truth for its own sake, think much less of property in truth. They accept it thankfully everywhere, and do not label or stamp it with any man's name, for it is theirs long beforehand, and from eternity. The learned and the studious of thought have no monopoly of wisdom. Their violence of direction in some degree disqualifies them to think truly. We owe many valuable observations to people who are not very acute or profound, and who say the thing without effort which we want and have long been hunting in vain. The action of the soul is oftener in that which is felt and left unsaid than in that which is said in any conversation. It broods over every society, and they unconsciously seek for it in each other. We know better than we do. We do not yet possess ourselves, and we know at the same time that we are much more. I feel the same truth how often in my trivial conversation with my neighbors, that somewhat higher in each of us over-

looks this by-play, and Jove nods to Jove from behind each of us.

8. We esteem nations important, until we discover that a few individuals much more concern us; then, later, that it is not at last a few individuals, or any sacred heroes, but the lowliness, the outpouring, the large equality to truth of a single mind,—as if in the narrow walls of a human heart the whole realm of truth, the world of morals, the tribunal by which the universe is judged, found room to exist.

9. Mankind at large always resemble frivolous children: they are impatient of thought, and wish to be amused. Truth is too simple for us; we do not like those who unmask our illusions. Fontenelle said: "If the Deity should lay bare to the eyes of men the secret system of Nature, the causes by which all the astronomic results are affected, and they finding no magic, no mystic numbers, no fatalities, but the greatest simplicity, I am persuaded they would not be able to suppress a feeling of mortification, and would exclaim, with disappointment, 'Is that all?'" And so we paint over the bareness of ethics with the quaint grotesques of theology.

10. Heaven always bears some proportion to earth. The god of the cannibals will be a cannibal, of the crusaders a crusader, and of the

merchants a merchant. In all ages, souls out of time, extraordinary, prophetic, are born, who are rather related to the system of the world than to their particular age and locality. These announce absolute truths, which, with whatever reverence received, are speedily dragged down into a savage interpretation.

11. It is the curious property of truth to be uncontainable and ever enlarging. Truth indeed! We talk as if we had it, or sometimes said it, or knew anything about it,—that terrific re-agent. 'Tis a gun with a recoil which will knock down the most nimble artillerists, and therefore is never fired. The ideal is as far ahead of the videttes of the van as it is of the rear. And before the good we aim at, all history is symptomatic, and only a good omen.

12. All science has one aim, namely, to find a theory of nature. We have theories of races and of functions, but scarcely yet a remote approach to an idea of creation. We are now so far from the road to truth, that religious teachers dispute and hate each other, and speculative men are esteemed unsound and frivolous. But to a sound judgment, the most abstract truth is the most practical. Whenever a true theory appears, it will be its own evidence. Its test is, that it will explain all phenomena.

13. He that speaks the truth executes no

private function of an individual will, but the
world utters a sound by his lips. He who doth
a just action seeth therein nothing of his own,
but an inconceivable nobleness attaches to it,
because it is a dictate of the general mind. We
have no idea of power so simple and so entire
as this. It is the basis of thought, it is the basis
of being. Compare all that we call ourselves, all
our private and personal venture in the world,
with this deep or moral nature in which we lie,
and our private good becomes an impertinence,
and we take part with hasty shame against ourselves:—

"High instincts, before which our mortal na-
        ture
  Doth tremble like a guilty thing surprised,—
  Which, be they what they may,
  Are yet the fountain-light of all our day,
  Are yet the master-light of all our seeing,—
  Uphold us, cherish, and have power to make
  Our noisy years seem moments in the being
  Of the eternal silence,—truths that wake
  To perish never."

    14. Where but in the intuitions which are
vouchsafed us from within, shall we learn the
Truth? Faithless, faithless, we fancy that with
the dust we depart and are not, and do not know
that the law and the perception of the law are
at last one; that only as much as the law enters

us, becomes us, we are living men,—immortal with the immortality of this law. Underneath all these appearances lies that which is, that which lives, that which causes. This ever renewing generation of appearances rests on a reality, and a reality that is alive.

15. Be content with a little light, so it be your own. Explore, and explore. Be neither chided nor flattered out of your position of perpetual inquiry. Neither dogmatize, nor accept another's dogmatism. Why should you renounce your right to traverse the star-lit deserts of Truth, for the premature comforts of an acre, house, and barn? Truth also has its roof, and bed, and board. Make yourself necessary to the world, and mankind will give you bread . . .

Immortality

1. I am a better believer, and all serious souls are better believers in the immortality, than we can give grounds for. The real evidence is too subtle, or is higher than we can write down in propositions, and therefore Wordsworth's Ode is the best modern essay on the subject.

2. A man of thought is willing to die, willing to live; I suppose because he has seen the thread on which the beads are strung, and perceived that it reaches up and down, existing quite independently of the present illusions. A man of affairs is afraid to die, is pestered with

terrors, because he has not this vision, and is the
victim of those who have moulded the religious
doctrines into some neat and plausible system
. . . for household use. It is the fear of the young
bird to trust its wings. The experiences of the
soul will fast outgrow this alarm. The saying
of Marcus Antoninus it were hard to mend: "It
is well to die if there be gods, and sad to live if
there be none." I think all sound minds rest on
a certain preliminary conviction, namely, that
if it be best that conscious personal life shall
continue, it will continue; if not best, then it
will not: and we, if we saw the whole, should
of course see that it was better so.

3. Of immortality, the soul when well em-
ployed is incurious. It is so well, that it is sure
it will be well. It asks no questions of the Supreme Power. . . . 'Tis a higher thing to confide
that if it is best we should live, we shall live,—
'tis higher to have this conviction than to have
the lease of indefinite centuries and millenniums
and aeons. Higher than the question of our
duration is the question of our deserving. Immortality will come to such as are fit for it, and
he who would be a great soul in future must be
a great soul now. It is a doctrine too great to
rest on any legend, that is, on any man's experience but our own. It must be proved, if at
all, from our own activity and designs, which

imply an interminable future for their play.

4. Do not require a description of the countries towards which you sail. The description does not describe them to you, and to-morrow you arrive there and know them by inhabiting them. Men ask concerning the immortality of the soul, the employments of heaven, the state of the sinner, and so forth. They even dream that Jesus has left replies to precisely these interrogatories. Never a moment did that sublime spirit speak in their *patois.* To truth, justice, love, the attributes of the soul, the idea of immutableness is essentially associated. Jesus, living in these moral sentiments, heedless of sensual fortunes, heeding only the manifestations of these, never made the separation of the idea of duration from the essence of these attributes, nor uttered a syllable concerning the duration of the soul. It was left to his disciples to sever duration from the moral elements, and to teach the immortality of the soul as a doctrine, and maintain it by evidences. The moment the doctrine of the immortality is separately taught, man is already fallen. In the flowing of love, in the adoration of humility, there is no question of continuance. No inspired man ever asks this question or condescends to these evidences. For the soul is true to itself, and the man in whom it is shed abroad cannot wander from the pres-

ent, which is infinite, to a future which would be finite.

5. Sufficient to to-day are the duties of to-day. Don't waste life in doubts and fears; spend yourself on the work before you, well assured that the right performance of this hour's duties will be the best preparation for the hours or ages that follow it:—

"The name of death was never terrible
To him that knew to live."

Christianity

*The words that I speak unto you I speak not
of myself, but the Father that dwelleth in me.*

The kingdom of God is within you.

*Why callest thou me good? There is none
good but one, that is, God.*

*The works that I do shall he do also; and
greater works than these shall he do.*

Thus spake Jesus of Nazareth.

1. Jesus Christ belonged to the true race
of prophets. He saw with open eye the mystery
of the soul. Drawn by its severe harmony,
ravished with its beauty, he lived in it, and had
his being there. Alone in all history he esti-

mated the greatness of man. One man was true
to what is in you and me. He saw that God in-
carnates himself in man, and evermore goes
forth anew to take possession of his World. He
said, in this jubilee of sublime emotion, 'I am
divine. Through me, God acts; through me,
speaks. Would you see God, see me; or see thee,
when thou also thinkest as I now think.' But
what a distortion did his doctrine and memory
suffer in the same, in the next, and the following ages!

2. He felt respect for Moses and the prophets, but no unfit tenderness at postponing their
initial revelations to the hour and the man that
now is; to the eternal revelation in the heart.
Thus was he a true man. Having seen that the
law in us is commanding, he would not suffer
it to be commanded. Boldly, with hand, and
heart, and life, he declared it was God. Thus
is he, as I think, the only soul in history who
has appreciated the worth of man.

3. In this point of view we become sensible
of the first defect of historical Christianity.
Historical Christianity has fallen into the error
that corrupts all attempts to communicate religion. As it appears to us, and as it has appeared for ages, it is not the doctrine of the
soul, but an exaggeration of the personal, the
positive, the ritual. It has dwelt, it dwells, with

noxious exaggeration about the *person* of Jesus.

4. All who hear me, feel that the language that describes Christ to Europe and America is not the style of friendship and enthusiasm to a good and noble heart, but is appropriated and formal . . . Accept the injurious impositions of our early catechetical instruction, and even honesty and self-denial were but splendid sins, if they did not wear the Christian name.
One would rather be
"A pagan, suckled in a creed outworn,"
than to be defrauded of his manly right in coming into nature and finding . . . even virtue and truth foreclosed and monopolized. You shall not be a man even. . . . you shall not dare and live after the infinite Law that is in you, and in company with the infinite Beauty which heaven and earth reflect to you in all lovely forms; but you must subordinate your nature to Christ's nature; you must accept our interpretations, and take his portrait as the vulgar draw it.

5. That is always best which gives me to myself. The sublime is excited in me by the great stoical doctrine, Obey thyself. That which shows God in me, fortifies me. That which shows God out of me, makes me a wart and a wen. There is no longer a necessary reason for my being.

6. The divine bards are the friends of my

virtue, of my intellect, of my strength. . . . So I love them. Noble provocations go out from them, inviting me to resist evil; to subdue the world; and to Be. And thus, by his holy thoughts, Jesus serves us, and thus only. To aim to convert a man by miracles is a profanation of the soul. A true conversion, a true Christ, is now, as always, to be made by the reception of beautiful sentiments. It is true that a great and rich soul, like his, falling among the simple, does so preponderate, that, as his did, it names the world. The world seems to them to exist for him, and they have not yet drunk so deeply of his sense as to see that only by coming again to themselves, or to God in themselves, can they grow forevermore.

7. I feel myself pledged, if health and opportunity be granted me, to demonstrate that all necessary truth is its own evidence; that no doctrine of God need appeal to a book; that Christianity is wrongly received by all such as take it for a system of doctrines,—its stress being upon moral truth; it is a rule of life, not a rule of faith.

8. The Belief in Christianity that now prevails is the Unbelief of men. They will have Christ for a Lord and not for a Brother. Christ preaches the greatness of man, but we hear only the greatness of Christ.

9. The second defect of the traditionary and limited way of using the mind of Christ is a consequence of the first; this, namely; that the Moral Nature, that Law of laws whose revelations introduce greatness—yea, God himself—into the open soul, is not explored as the fountain of the established teaching in society. Men have come to speak of the revelation as somewhat long ago given and done, as if God were dead. The injury to faith throttles the preacher; and the goodliest of institutions becomes an uncertain and inarticulate voice.

10. My friends, in these two errors, I think, I find the causes of a decaying church and a wasting unbelief. And what greater calamity can fall upon a nation than the loss of worship? Then all things go to decay. Genius leaves the temple to haunt the senate or the market. Literature becomes frivolous. Science is cold. The eye of youth is not lighted by the hope of other worlds, and age is without honor.

11. The stationariness of religion; the assumption that the age of inspiration is past, that the Bible is closed; the fear of degrading the character of Jesus by representing him as a man; —indicate with sufficient clearness the falsehood of our theology. It is the office of a true teacher to show us that God is, not was; that He speaketh, not spake. The true Christianity,

—a faith like Christ's in the infinitude of man,
—is lost. None believeth in the soul of man,
but only in some man or person old' and de-
parted. Ah me! no man goeth alone. All men
go in flocks to this saint or that poet, avoiding
the God who seeth in secret. They cannot see
in secret; they love to be blind in public. They
think society wiser than their soul, and know
not that one soul, and their soul, is wiser than
the whole world.

12. Look at it how we will, the most wonderful fact in history is Christianity; the fact
that ten or twenty persons . . . did receive, con-
sciously or unconsciously, the revelations of the
moral sentiment, with such depth and tenacity
as to live and die in and for them, and to propa-
gate their statement each one to so wide a circle
of contemporaries, and then to the next age,
that the enthusiasm got a footing in the world
and throve and grew into this great Christen-
dom we know so well.

13. I believe the Christian religion to be
profoundly true,—true to an extent that they
who are styled its most orthodox defenders have
never, or but in rarest glimpses once or twice
in a lifetime, reached. I am for the principles;
they are for the men. They reckon me unbe-
lieving; I, with better reason, them. They mag-
nify inspiration, miracles, mediatorship, the

Trinity, baptism, and eucharist. I let them all drop in sight of the glorious beauty of those inward laws or harmonies which ravished the eye of Jesus, of Socrates, of Plato, of Dante, of Milton, of George Fox, of Swedenborg.

14. I have no curiosity respecting historical Christianity; respecting persons and miracles: I take the phenomenon as I find it, and let it have its effect on me, careless whether it is a poem or a chronicle.

15. It is because the Bible wears black cloth. It comes with a certain official claim against which the mind revolts. The book has its own nobilities—might well be charming, if it was left simply on its merits, as the others; but this 'you must',—'it is your duty', repels. 'Tis like the introduction of martial law into Concord. If you should dot our farms with picket lines, and I could not go or come across lots without a pass, I should resist, or else emigrate.

16. With each new mind, a new secret of nature transpires; nor can the Bible be closed until the last great man is born.

17. I look for the hour when that Supreme Beauty which ravished the souls of those Eastern men, and chiefly of those Hebrews, and through their lips spoke oracles to all time, shall speak in the West also. The Hebrew and Greek Scriptures contain immortal sentences, that have

been bread of life to millions. But they have no epical integrity; are fragmentary; are not shown in their order to the intellect. I look for the new Teacher that shall follow so far those shining laws that he shall see them come full circle; shall see their rounding complete grace; shall see the world to be the mirror of the soul; shall see the identity of the law of gravitation with purity of heart; and shall show that the Ought, that Duty, is one thing with Science, with Beauty, and with Joy.

18. The world is young: the former great men call to us affectionately. We too must write Bibles, to unite again the heavens and the earthly world. The secret of genius is to suffer no fiction to exist for us; to realize all that we know; in the high refinement of modern life, in arts, in sciences, in books, in men, to exact good faith, reality and a purpose; and first, last, midst and without end, to honor every truth by use.

19. Christianity is rightly dear to the best of mankind; yet was there never a young philosopher whose breeding had fallen into the Christian church by whom that brave text of Paul's was not specially prized: "Then shall also the Son be subject unto Him who put all things under him, that God may be all in all."

God

1. Do not speak of God much. After a very little conversation on the highest nature, thought deserts us and we run into formalism.

2. It pains me never that I cannot give you an accurate answer to the question, What is God? What is the operation we call Providence? and the like. There lies the answer: there it exists, present, omnipresent to you, to me.

3. Personality and impersonality might each be affirmed of Absolute Being; and what may not be affirmed of it in our own mind? And when we have heaped a mountain of speeches, we have still to begin again, having

nowise expressed the simple unalterable fact.

4. Beware of interference. Direct service
the God reserves to himself. The condition of
greatness, that is of health, is poise; and reception only from the Soul; illustration from
men, but reception only from God through Self.

5. God never speaks by a third person, for
he is nearer than the nearest. You exist from
him. It is as if some one came from the other
side of the planet to tell me what I thought.
We inhabit a thousand and a thousand planes.
Go home now to thy closet, to thy heart, to
Being, and listen. Go, that is, and sit and ascer-
tain what truth of you this man fantastically
said, but yet said, and subtract what vast
amounts of individualism have mixed with that
pure universalism that is yours as well as his,
neither yours nor his, but Being's.

6. Let man learn . . . that the Highest
dwells with him . . . If he would know what
the great God speaketh, he must 'go into his
closet and shut the door,' as Jesus said. God
will not make himself manifest to cowards. He
must greatly listen to himself, withdrawing himself from all the accents of other men's de-
votion. Even their prayers are hurtful to him,
until he have made his own. Our religion vul-
garly stands on numbers of believers. Whenever the appeal is made,—no matter how in-

directly,—to numbers, proclamation is then and there made that religion is not. He that finds God a sweet enveloping thought to him never counts his company. When I sit in that presence, who shall dare to come in? When I rest in perfect humility, when I burn with pure love, what can Calvin or Swedenborg say?

7. The infallible index of true progress is found in the tone the man takes. Neither his age, nor his breeding, nor company, nor books, nor actions, nor talents, nor all together can hinder him from being deferential to a higher spirit than his own. If he have not found his home in God, his manners, his forms of speech, the turn of his sentences, the build, shall I say, of all his opinions will involuntarily confess it, let him brave it out how he will. If he have found his centre, the Deity will shine through him, through all the disguises of ignorance, of ungenial temperament, of unfavorable circumstance. The tone of seeking is one, and the tone of having is another.

8. The faith that stands on authority is not faith. The reliance on authority measures the decline of religion, the withdrawal of the soul.

9. The only money of God is God. He pays never with anything less or anything else. The only reward of virtue is virtue . . .

10. Will is the measure of power. To a

great genius there must be a great will. If the thought is not a lamp to the will, does not proceed to an act, the wise are imbecile. He alone is strong and happy who has a will. The rest are herds. He uses; they are used. He is of the Maker; they are of the Made.

11. Will is always miraculous, being the presence of God to men. When it appears in a man he is a hero, and all metaphysics are at fault. Heaven is the exercise of the faculties, the added sense of power.

12. Morals is the direction of the will on universal ends.

13. The exercise of the Will, or the lesson of power, is taught in every event. From the child's successive possession of his several senses up to the hour when he saith, "Thy will be done!" he is learning the secret that he can reduce under his will not only particular events but great classes, nay, the whole series of events, and so conform all facts to his character. Nature is thoroughly mediate. It is made to serve. It receives the dominion of man as meekly as the ass on which the Saviour rode. It offers all its kingdoms to man as the raw material which he may mould into what is useful.

14. In what prayers do men allow themselves! That which they call a holy office is not so much as brave and manly. Prayer looks

abroad and asks for some foreign addition to come through some foreign virtue, and loses itself in endless mazes of natural and supernatural, and mediatorial and miraculous. Prayer that craves a particular commodity, anything less than all good, is vicious. Prayer is the contemplation of the facts of life from the highest point of view. It is the soliloquy of a beholding and jubilant soul. It is the spirit of God pronouncing his works good. But prayer as a means to effect a private end is meanness and theft. It supposes dualism and not unity in nature and consciousness. As soon as the man is at one with God, he will not beg. He will then see prayer in all action.

15. Is not prayer also a study of truth,— a sally of the soul into the unfound infinite? No man ever prayed heartily without learning something. But when a faithful thinker, resolute to detach every object from personal relations and see it in the light of thought, shall, at the same time, kindle science with the fire of the holiest affections, then will God go forth anew into the creation.

16. The Religion that is afraid of science dishonours God and commits suicide.

17. A sect or party is an elegant incognito devised to save a man from the vexation of thinking.

18. The lines of the religious sects are very shifting; their platforms unstable; the whole science of theology of great uncertainty, and resting very much on the opinions of who may chance to be the leading doctors of Oxford or Edinburgh, of Princeton or Cambridge, to-day.

19. Theological problems . . . never presented a practical difficulty to any man,—never darkened across any man's road who did not go out of his way to seek them. These are the soul's mumps and measles and whooping-coughs . . . A simple mind will not know these enemies. It is quite another thing that he should be able to give account of his faith and expound to another the theory of his self-union and freedom.

20. Thus all concentrates: let us not rove; let us sit at home with the cause. Let us stun and astonish the intruding rabble of men and books and institutions by a simple declaration of the divine fact. Bid the invaders take the shoes from off their feet, for God is here within.

21. Let a man believe in God, and not in names and places and persons.

22. O my brothers, God exists. There is a soul at the centre of nature and over the will of every man, so that none of us can wrong the universe. It has so infused its strong enchantment into nature that we prosper when we ac-

cept its advice, and when we struggle to wound
its creatures our hands are glued to our sides,
or they beat our own breasts. The whole course
of things goes to teach us faith. We need only
obey. There is guidance for each of us, and by
lowly listening we shall hear the right word.
Why need you choose so painfully your place
and occupation and associates and modes of
action and of entertainment? Certainly there is
a possible right for you that precludes the need
of balance and wilful election. For you there is
a reality, a fit place and congenial duties. Place
yourself in the middle of the stream of power
and wisdom which animates all whom it floats,
and you are without effort impelled to truth, to
right and a perfect contentment. Then you put
all gainsayers in the wrong. Then you are the
world, the measure of right, of truth, of beauty.
If we would not be mar-plots with our miserable
interferences, the work, the society, letters, arts,
science, religion of men would go on far better
than now, and the heaven predicted from the
beginning of the world, and still predicted from
the bottom of the heart, would organize itself,
as do now the rose and the air and the sun.

23. The soul that ascends to worship the
great God is plain and true; has no rose-color,
no fine friends, no chivalry, no adventures;
does not want admiration; dwells in the hour

that now is, in the earnest experience of the common day,—by reason of the present moment and the mere trifle having become porous to thought and bibulous of the sea of light.

24.　Ineffable is the union of man and God in every act of the soul. The simplest person who in his integrity worships God, becomes God; yet for ever and ever the influx of this better and universal self is new and unsearchable. It inspires awe and astonishment. How dear, how soothing to man, arises the idea of God, peopling the lonely place, effacing the scars of our mistakes and disappointments! When we have broken our god of tradition and ceased from our god of rhetoric, then may God fire the heart with his presence.

25.　Self-reliance, the height and perfection of man, is reliance on God.

The Individual

1. In all my lectures, I have taught one doctrine, namely, the infinitude of the private man.

2. Souls are not saved in bundles.

3. Leave this hypocritical prating about the masses. Masses are rude, unmade, pernicious in their demands and influence . . . I wish not to concede anything to them, but to . . . divide and break them up, and draw individuals out of them.

4. The only progress ever known was of the individual.

5. I cannot find language of sufficient en-

ergy to convey my sense of the sacredness of private integrity. All men, all things, the state, the church, yea, the friends of the heart are phantasms and unreal beside the sanctuary of the heart.

6. The less government we have the better, —the fewer laws, and the less confided power. The antidote to this abuse of formal government is the influence of private character, the growth of the Individual . . .

7. The excess of individualism, when it is not corrected or subordinated to the Supreme Reason, makes that vice which we stigmatize as monotones, men of one idea, . . . which give such a comic tinge to all society. Every man has his theory, true, but ridiculously overstated. We are forced to treat a great part of mankind as if they were a little deranged.

8. The impoverishing philosophy of ages has laid stress on the distinctions of the individual, and not on the universal attributes of man.

9. We are taught by great actions that the universe is the property of every individual in it. Every rational creature has all nature for his dowry and estate. It is his, if he will. He may divest himself of it; he may creep into a corner, and abdicate his kingdom, as most men do, but he is entitled to the world by his constitution.

In proportion to the energy of his thought and will, he takes up the world into himself.

10. Every thing that tends to insulate the individual,—to surround him with barriers of natural respect, so that each man shall feel the world is his, and man shall treat with man as a sovereign state with a sovereign state,—tends to true union as well as greatness.

11. The world is nothing, the man is all; in yourself is the law of all nature, and you know not yet how a globule of sap ascends; in yourself slumbers the whole of Reason; it is for you to know all; it is for you to dare all.

12. Character is . . . moral order seen through the medium of an individual nature. An individual is an encloser. Time and space, liberty and necessity, truth and thought, are left at large no longer.

13. Is it not the chief disgrace in the world, not to be an unit;—not to be reckoned one character;—not to yield that peculiar fruit which each man was created to bear, but to be reckoned in the gross, in the hundred, or the thousand, of the party, the section, to which we belong; and our opinion predicted geographically, as the north, or the south? Not so, brothers and friends—please God, ours shall not be so. We will walk on our own feet; we will work with our own hands; we will speak our own

minds. . . . A nation of men will for the first time exist, because each believes himself inspired by the Divine Soul which also inspires all men.

14. In the soul then let the redemption be sought. Wherever a man comes, there comes revolution. The old is for slaves. When a man comes, all books are legible, all things transparent, all religions are forms. He is religious. Man is the wonder-worker.

15. When I wish, it is permitted me to say, These hands, this body, this history of Waldo Emerson are profane and wearisome, but I, I descend not to mix myself with that or with any man. Above his life, above all creatures, I flow down forever a sea of benefit into races of individuals. Nor can the stream ever roll backward or the sin or death of a man taint the immutable energy which distributes itself into men, as the sun into rays, or the sea into drops.

The Voice at Eve

Here was a man. A simple, humble and virtuous citizen of Concord. He had no panacea for society. He never attempted to fix Truth. He wanted to bring men "not to me, but to themselves." He urged men to "be real and admirable, not as we know, but as you know." He simply reported "what hints I have collected of the transcendent simplicity and energy of the Highest Law." He pondered the attributes of God and found them all good. His affections and intellect were equally developed, as Thoreau noted. It was mind as well as heart, wisdom as well as humanity, that moved him to say:

I am primarily engaged to myself to be a public servant of all the gods, to demonstrate to all men that there is intelligence and good will at the heart of things, and ever higher and yet higher leadings.

Being thus dedicated, it is natural to find him saying:

Do not set the least value on what I do, or the least discredit on what I do not, as if I pretended to settle any thing as true or false. I unsettle all things. No facts are to me sacred; none are profane; I simply experiment, an endless seeker with no Past at my back.

A man, yes—Waldo Emerson. But also a Prophet who descended not to mix himself with Waldo Emerson or with any man. He dealt a stunning blow to soulless Tradition. He exposed the folklore of a faltering civilization. He laid the foundation for a new and more excellent society than history has recorded. He pointed man to the Supreme Spirit in his own soul. He smashed a neurotic pessimism that has no hope because it has no vision. "We grant that human life is mean, but how did we find out that it was mean?"

There is a difference between one and another hour of life in their authority and subsequent effect. Our faith comes in moments; our vice is habitual. Yet there is a depth in those brief moments which constrains us to ascribe more reality to them than to all other experiences.

How did we find out that life is mean? In the very fact that we did lies the hope of a new day. We are disturbed by things that former centuries accepted as a normal part of the status quo. Can it be that the Moral Sentiment is more sensitive? Can it be that we are more intolerant of hypocrisy, deceit, rationalization and all of the other negative aspects of life?

In the solitude to which every man is always returning, he has a sanity and revelations which in his passage into new worlds he will carry with him. Never mind the ridicule, never mind the defeat; up again, old heart!—it seems to say,—there is victory yet for all justice; and the true romance which the world exists to realize will be the transformation of genius into practical power.

We are passing into a New World. The Spirit will be enthroned in the heart of man. Then will come a philosophy of insight and out of that the transformation of genius into practical power. Then a new economics, a government based on morality, an education that develops the whole man, a humanized science and a religion that is Religion.

To all this we are pointed by this Prophet

*who flows down forever a sea of benefit into
races of individuals. When the Call came he
was ready. He had obeyed "the voice at eve
obeyed at prime." He had not professed that
which he did not believe. Nor had he heeded
the voice of man when it agreed not with the
voice of God in his own soul. He had studied
and obeyed the laws of the universe. And the
life of the soul in conscious union with the
Infinite had been for him the only real existence.*

*To his fellow countrymen he had preached
the gospel of the New World!*

*Henry Thoreau was not given to sentiment.
But, thinking of this Prophet, he was moved to
say to his Journal: "There is no such general
critic of men and things, no such trustworthy
and faithful man. More of the divine realized
in him than in any."*

*Thus wrote Thoreau in youthful exuberance.
But at eve the Prophet created the same impression. Walt Whitman came near the end and
beheld "a just man, poised on himself, all-lov-
ing, all-enclosing, and sane and clear as the sun."*

*Qualis ab incepto. The same as from the be-
ginning. The Prophet is immovably centred.*

The sun set; but set not his hope:
Stars rose; his faith was earlier up:
Fixed on the enormous galaxy,

Deeper and older seemed his eye;
And matched his sufferance sublime
The taciturnity of time.
He spoke, and words more soft than rain
Brought the Age of Gold again.

SOURCES

Key:

C. —Centenary Edition of Emerson's Works, 12 volumes, Houghton Mifflin (first number indicates volume and second number the page—i. e. C. 10-120 refers to Centenary Edition, volume 10, page 120).

J. —Journals of Ralph Waldo Emerson, 10 volumes, Houghton Mifflin.

H.J.—The Heart of Emerson's Journals, edited by Bliss Perry, Houghton Mifflin.
Names of better known essays, poems and addresses, most likely to appear in other volumes, are given.

NOTE

In the final chapter Thoreau's remarks appear on page 45 of "The Heart of Thoreau's Journals", edited by Odell Shepard (Houghton Mifflin). Whenever possible I have referred to "The Heart of Emerson's Journals," as this book is accessible to more readers.

The complete text of the creed quoted on page 7 may be found in the biography of Emerson by Oliver Wendell Holmes (pp. 370-371). Two authorities incline to the view that Emerson did not write this creed, that Dr. Holmes used these words, to quote one authority, "as an effective figurative means of summarizing what he thought Emerson's basic convictions were by about 1832."

On the other hand, Dr. Samuel Crothers quotes this creed on the final page of his work on Emerson, and comments on it as follows: "While a young man, he (Emerson) had written down certain resolutions by which he wished to guide his life."

Newton Dillaway

Wakefield, Mass.

127

UNITY SCHOOL OF CHRISTIANITY
Unity Village, MO 64065

Printed U.S.A.

35-25C-2-91